BEYOND ELSEWHERE

BEYOND ELSEWHERE

Gabriel Arnou-Laujeac

Translated from the French
by Hélène Cardona

WHITE PINE PRESS / BUFFALO, NEW YORK

White Pine Press
P.O. Box 236 Buffalo, NY 14201
www.whitepine.org

Publication of this book was made possible, in part, by public funds from the New York State Council on the Arts, a State Agency.

White Pine Press appreciates the support of The French Ministry of Culture, the Institut Francais, and the Cultural Services of the French Embassy. *Beyond Elsewhere* is published thanks to a Hemingway Grant.

Library of Congress Control Number: 2015943682

ISBN: 978-1-935210-83-2

Gracious thanks to the following literary journals and anthologies where many excerpts first appeared, sometimes in different incarnations: *The London Magazine, Cha: An Asian Literary Journal, World Literature Today, Tabula Poetica, National Translation Month, Poetry East-West, Fjords Review, Fulcrum: An Anthology of Poetry and Aesthetics, The Enchanting Verses Literary Review, The Original Van Gogh's Ear Anthology, Life and Legends, Levure Littéraire, Francopolis,* and *Asian Signature.*

Deep gratitude to Christopher Merrill, Sidney Wade, Victoria Chang, Willis Barnstone, and John FitzGerald for their inspiration and support, and to Dennis Maloney, Elaine LaMattina, and Robert Alexander at White Pine Press for delivering this book into the world.

INTRODUCTION

Beyond Elsewhere is a verse narrative that speaks of exile. It is the odyssey of a soul in search of the absolute, the epiphany of being in love that represents a moment in eternity, at once of distress and salvation, a beacon on one's path. As poet Maram Al-Masri (Prix international de poésie Antonio Viccaro, Prix de la Société des Gens de Lettres), asserts in the preface to the French edition, one enters into Gabriel Arnou-Laujeac's world "as one enters an ancient forest, a temple, a pagoda — a place, not of religion, but of intense spirituality."

Beyond Elsewhere is a journey beyond space and time, a wide-open window into the invisible. We travel from life's beginning beyond the known world in a quest for the divine, to meet the other and oneself, in search of infinite love. It is a hauntingly beautiful long prose poem, a dance that at once touches on the universal and uniquely personal. With his debut collection, Gabriel Arnou-Laujeac establishes himself as one of French poetry's most innovative new voices. His retelling of a first mad love is lyrical, masterful, and exquisite, an opening into the elusive, affirming the absolute necessity of listening to the world. *Beyond Elsewhere* is a symphonic poem with boundless language, where past and present meet.

Poetry's essence is to capture our sense of awe and the ineffable. We write to expand our consciousness. Critic Alain Santacreu avers in *Contrelittérature* that "Gabriel Arnou-Laujeac is one of those 'horrible workers' Rimbaud spoke of, one of those poets whose quest begins on the horizon where others have collapsed. His writing is marked by the heartbreaking melancholy of the auroral state, a poetic and mystical language in which the soul becomes memory: memory of oneself as an image of God. Subjective, not preformed, his narrative poem rejects formalism, taking a poetic prose released from the line itself, with no other typography than the prospect of meaning and depth."

Gabriel Arnou-Laujeac's distinctive voice, elegiac and luminous, follows the lineage of Hafez, Rumi, and Tagore. In *Recours au Poème*, Michel Cazenave, philosopher, novelist, poet, literary critic and producer of the cult radio show *The Living and the Gods*, declares Arnou-Laujeac to be "a poet of rare magnitude, who takes us on steep roads where we breathe the fresh mountain air — and where we rediscover what is expected of poetry, which, according to its etymology, is to create a universe while revealing it, and where we can only find ourselves in the end."

Beyond Elsewhere brings to mind Baudelaire's prose poems and philosophy. As Baudelaire proclaims in the preface to *Le Spleen de Paris*, "Who among us has not, in his days of ambition, dreamed the miracle of a poetic prose, musical without rhythm and rhyme, sufficiently flexible and uneven to adapt to the lyrical movements of the soul, the undulations of reverie, the jolts of consciousness?"

Arnou-Laujeac expresses the alchemy of grace, allowing the work to become a spell, a hymn to love. French critic Sylvie Besson, Ph.D., states in *Le Nouveau Recueil* that in this narrative poem "everything brings us back, indeed, to the past, the source, oceanic feeling, before-world, beyond language. Gabriel Arnou-Laujeac's poetry conveys a wild carnal and sensual body, animal and glorious, a body of extraordinary perception, distancing itself precisely, good for him, from all the suffering, melancholy and despair, all the black visions, sadness, pain. There is in that body something indefinable, which also sets him apart from the sole pursuit of happiness to move toward a very acute sense of liturgy, something that has the power of a new gospel, something which completely changes the dimension of language, a mystical eloquence, an incantatory song, a musical climax that makes *Beyond Elsewhere* a singular and without any doubt unique work."

And Jean-Luc Maxence, poet, writer and publisher (Le Nouvel Athanor), tells us that "unparalleled psalms, forbidden hymns exist in Gabriel Arnou-Laujeac's unusual and sacred way of dying in 'this inverted world.' This is often of an almost liturgical beauty."

"Translation is a kind of transubstantiation; one poem becomes another," writes Anne Michaels. The translator is an intermediary, a technician, magician and alchemist working between languages to create inspired texts spanning cultural differences, geographic distances, and time. *Plus loin qu'ailleurs* was a challenge in many ways, with its concise and exacting style, lyricism, play on words, and spiritual dimension. Translation is a craft. It is also an inspired act, a negotiation. To quote Henry James, "we work in the dark," from that intuitive place. It becomes an act of revelation, the ultimate act of sympathy.

—Hélène Cardona

Passages from this text were published in *World Literature Today.* ("Translation as a Love Affair: *Beyond Elsewhere*, by Gabriel Arnou-Laujeac," 2015).

BEYOND ELSEWHERE

To my daughter, Olivia

Exiled, you rule on the expanse,
Immensity, childhood resembles you,
Heart torn, broken, you gather us,
O plenitude, I adore you naked.

—Jean Mambrino

Before disappearing far off, farther than the human eye could launch its arrow, the gods shook the firmament, let fall a few fragments of infinity on my forehead, and breathed the nostalgia of the Absolute into my core. A blazing firebrand planted in the soft flesh, from birth: echoes of silence striking my chest; presence within absence, sprung from the ocean of ages like a wave of equinox. How could I bear to be abandoned to the chimeras of fate, to be promised to the twilight of a dark age by the brightest light?

Wherever I turned my face, I only saw a world of shadowy temples and the specter of the absence covering every atom of the universe: herds roaming the surface of the earth, their foreheads hitting the walls of a trompe-l'oeil labyrinth; dwarf shepherds, bloated with bad winds, demoralizing the masses to better control them; anonymous hands diverting the great wheel of history in the cold rooms of power; "bull-faced Stupidity" — old, ugly and controlling — ordering heaven's dark stars and four winds emptied of their God.

This century without sky and anchor was only a mirage; this sprinkling of sand thrown into the ocean of existence, but a fable: it was not me. I knew it. I felt it. No matter what I did, I remained a spectator; no matter what I saw, a stranger to the spectacle. These hordes of undead staggering over the void gave me vertigo. All this warm flesh drunk with the wine of oblivion nauseated me. Everything was too ugly to be true. I prayed to be torn from Man's long sleep, to be offered love and truth blended with the eternal present. I would have liked the seemingly real to fall like a veil at the foot of a larger Reality, to burn there on the spot: forever.

Dreams of Elsewhere. Dreams of beyond elsewhere. My lungs were seeking the high seas air, the one that is sorely lacking.

So the eye, astray on a wide beach,
Sees the fugitive waves recede from the shore,
Decrease, flatten, soon only offering the eyes
A quiet horizon blended in the skies.

—Louis Raymond de Carbonnières

The first love wards off the specter of a world inhabited by rusty-winged adults with collapsed dreams, whose automated arms open before you but no longer close. It takes the place of worldly theater, of a societal lie, of a future with deserted temples and a wrinkled forehead. Curtain. Give way to the sun. To all the rising suns.

The light is here, with her.

She reveals herself to my gaze naturally, the way spring unveils the blueness of sky or the gold of your skin. She slowly removes makeup, masks and ornaments, and gives me a vision of herself bewitched, of herself bewitching: she adores me and I unlock her.

Sprung raw from a virginal flame, passion takes us whole under its animal breath: the sun sparks impale our bodies galloping in a crash of oceans.

We reign in this world where the beloved becomes everything, the only face of what is faceless, this shoreless elsewhere suddenly offering itself bare: we reign as servants of the first heartbreak given over to the fervor and dictatorship of our eighteen years.

Our bodies are wild swans alit on the river of desire, our hearts two waves rising to the ebb and flow of our eager breath, then diving back to their undivided source, burying space and time in the shifting sands of unfathomable abysses. The immensity calling me grants me the ocean, whole, in an embrace. And in my arms I have the same ocean for her. How can I but follow the occult wave pulling me far from earthly dampers, our Siamese bodies our only tie?

If infinity is unbridled, hers is a tie of blood and light, a bond of love that cannot be unraveled. This infinity is not neutral but feminine. It depends on the beloved to fulfill itself, but embodies a demiurgic power whose gods alone know the secret. What soul resists the intoxicating wine of love and the desire for the absolute quickened by the vine? What lovers don't harbor the memory of a plenitude to be reawakened, in the holy of holies of their intertwined bodies?

We are drunk; and our intoxication never falters: five years of insolent beauty, of insolated power, five years spanning a single day, one sleepless night, travelers without luggage on a continent without seasons, in the heat wave of perpetual summer.

And then comes the fall.

The pact with the heavens is broken. Paradise escapes beneath our feet: a cursed wind insists on making us fall from above ourselves, with implacable patience. Month after month, every stone of our imaginary temple collapses in a slow attack on reality.

With the last breath of passion, all that remains of our faces are fallen icons: two angelic visages torn by the blade of a love profaned to vestiges. Only our soulless faces and eyes remain, unable to withstand the vision of the fall. Only she and I remain: nothing. Nothing but the nausea whose sensation precedes the proclamation: the disenchantment.

The disenchantment is an earthquake. It sweeps the memory of what was sacred, of what makes everything, of what is no longer. It takes all away in its irresistible fall, even your shadow and light. It leaves you half dead, buried under the rubble of a rupture splitting the earth, in a solitude peopled by silent shadows: possession and addiction, euphoria and lack, fusion and absence are millennial drugs whose hunger is vast and whose end is devastating.

So much lost sky.

You dream of being the exception, but are just the rule: the first love empties your bag of marbles to fill it with stars, but this brutal flash carries within the lightning that ultimately blows them all out, one by one.

Love tucks you in bed one last time and gives you the big night kiss.

Why?

Why doesn't passion escape the tidal movement, the law of opposites, the back and forth between shadow and light, the imperturbable mechanical decline of all things here below?

I remain alone, without the soothing of a word, without the calming of a response. Words temporarily lose their magic, their magnificence. They are wingless birds, short-winded arrows that fall before reaching their target. I wander without her, in denial of her vain absence, like a ghost in the misleading immensity of temples in ruin.

I drift in silence, days and moons, on the sea of servitude that floods my every cell in mourning, before collapsing by the grace of time on the other shore of dead loves, drunk with the rolling of my shipwrecked pain. Rising, my back to the sea, facing the sun, I hear the wands of the future thrashing the drum of my heart, as if time, until now suspended in the relic of the past, again knocked at my door, ordering me to finally open it and resume our aborted dance.

I must spring forth from this unflappable throbbing — now. Regain the time lost looking for what no longer is, for what is not. Get up, rebuild myself in the void and urgency of a liberating despair: in the surrender of my illusions about the other, about me, about eternity. I now know human passion is exclusive, symbiotic, psychotropic, but that the key is the spell eluding it, the time that tears it to pieces.

I accept what is: what I believe to be. This white despair, paradoxical fruit of a vital impulse, delivers me from the prison of lack. Lack is there, but no longer here; at least I was burning to convince myself, with the impatience of those who still doubt.

Later, the rage to embrace the multitude spreads in the gold of my cells when I hear surging in my throat the absurd helpless cry tearing me from the long sleep of the senses:

"Since everything is transitory, I will love them all. And none."

Thus desire rekindles its torch for me, for my whole famished being.

I seek nothing, nothing known, nothing earthly. Celestial bodies, shooting stars, migratory breaths crossing the night without a trace. I seek nothing — everything — instant thousand faces never growing old, diverse bodies and gazes to deceive the emptiness of each.

In this game of mirrors, the quest for a sacred Lung — inspiring me since childhood — and my temptation to revive my whole being, strangely never fizzle. I remain the faithful shadow of an omnipresent light forever wandering, wrapping the final nakedness of my sleepless nights in a mystical shroud, and the temporary death of my body in illusory holiness. Every day God makes I spend the night sleepless; I light the gold of time with the fire of tempestuous ecstasies, and by the grace of ephemeral scorching beauties set the whole world ablaze in a bolt of eternity.

I take refuge in Woman's three jewels, her nine-gated temple and innumerable windows, renewing every night my vows of love in the sensual and relentless paradise of a wild liturgy.

Behind this bewitched mask, in rare lonely nights, I count conquest's faces, which I recite like a rosary: a rosary whose beads are their eyes, their many eyes staring at me, piercing me, transfixing me, flesh witnesses to my endless thirst, my inexhaustible hunger, accomplices I double-crossed. In their eyes I see myself with greatest clarity: an unhappy young man in search of endless love, who must first be without beginning to honor this condition.

I believe myself free of a future that creates absence and of hope that creates lack; but every morning the sun swallows the star asleep in my arms, stillborn in its milky ashes.

I hear love's throbbing beat behind the night curtain, but it never permeates. Love is covered in bashfulness. I hold her ghost in my arms, but never see her face. I run breathless behind her silhouette, but only her shadow appears. In truth I shun the heights of love, haunted by the memory of a vertiginous fall.

I wander in the desert of the world.

I drink the mirage water.

Gradually I understand. I gradually accept. I recall in my flesh Samuel Beckett's lines, in the somber and lucid heart of absence:

> *they come different and the same*
> *with each it is different and the same*
> *with each the absence of love is different*
> *with each the absence of love is the same.*

The absurd spreads its wings in the cage of existence. Its breath attempts to infiltrate the loophole of the body, seeking to possess me from the inside and make me the invalid priest of its inverted cult, cantor of a nihilist cry who chokes himself with terror as he jumps into the abyss.

I resist its misleading vertigo, its lying mirrors, its sick beauty. Through centuries of ancient glory to come, I am immune to the hissing snakebite of death nestled deep in the human soul. I stand beyond the borders of nothingness, outstretched toward the inaccessible.

I remember something else.

I remember a different plenitude of becoming and non-becoming, within everything and outside of everything, empty of everything but exempt of any emptiness. I remember a Kingdom that is neither here nor elsewhere, but which offers its love right here to those by emptiness abandoned.

I remember the All Other.

It was Me.

Me — by the grace of the All Other.

I now inhabit the refuge of night, a secret cabin in the soul, a space of grace and retreat. The tumult of the world recedes, for a few hours time is a ring on the finger of the Eternal: the seconds turn on themselves and form an unbroken circle, nothing can any more interrupt the inner music that carries me and takes me whole in its dervish dance. Traveling up the stream of inspiration toward its anonymous source, I hear the divine clamor, the echo of the first cry of ecstasy resounding since the dawn of all, rapt in the heart of the existential dream, the absurd, and grace.

I light the lamp of the invisible: she is here. Even invisible she is here; between words, in them, through them. She covers the entire page in shadow, ink, and light.

She is the rumor that rumbles at the bottom of the seashell stranded on the beach. Her beauty derives from elsewhere. She is the sun's song, the moon's sighs, an endless dream springing from the depths of another dream with a woman's bust and eagle wings: her, then me in her; her, then light.

She torments me, entrances me, she is the still virgin lover, the immaculate seat of an absolute vow that nothing earthly can fulfill. Even after starlit millennia within starlit millennia, she still is virgin, every day reinvented by the formula beyond the grave that lights the gold of time and the flame of our intangible bodies.

Her heady scent takes me in her Eastern palm and drops me in the loving shadow of her eyelashes, where immensity awaits. I breathe her; internalize her; become her: she is the sun's blood scabbing my skin, oxygen in my lungs, and my breath harmonizes with the high winds animating her.

Clad in space, with winds for belts, our naked bodies fly: from the sky, we reach the motionless center. We scour the heights of a borderless land, where ancient poets, dedicated to the worship of light, reign: their language is a sleepless flame, a fiery arrow pointing to the ineffable and to the other shore of the Real.

Her muse alphabet and soul-infused music lay bare in this place with no address, where we capsize from shadow to light, eyes closed, in the annihilation of all apparent realities. The illusion of being two no longer separates us. In truth, I am no longer here, nor is she. What remains is a soul divested of its two bodies, a light freed of shadow. Love remains at last reinvented beyond the damper of time, the prison of space, and the first seven heavens whose eighth she offers.

"I know a paradise that is a gateway to the stars, where one can drink the sun's blood, where one staggers naked on the back of constellations. I speak to you about over there, the horizon at the end of the shadow: toward clarity.

Come

I hold the keys to another world: a solar dynasty triumphing over the arbitrary as well as over dust.

Beyond this day-by-day too narrow for our wings exists a place toward the supreme star; and this is where I take you: toward clarity.

Come

I'll take you where the wind-people exile themselves, far from the despairing herd, away from its inhuman devils and too human gods.

I speak of the horizon at the end of silence: you will hear unparalleled psalms, forbidden hymns, songs that have always burned inside you.

Come

Beyond this day-by-day too narrow for our wings exists a place revealing the perfect supreme star; and this is where I take you: to Yourself."

I arrive.

In front of me, the sea. I contemplate the Horizon behind the horizon, where waves and ether marry. I'm a grain of sand in an ellipsis, a sun shard mingled with stardust haloing the still bare strand.

This is the absolute dawn.

The large azure bust stretches on the vast sea's sapphire bed. The elusive embraces the unfathomable in a long silence reflecting the ineffable. The sleepy-eyed Day awakens, spreads its ray, illuminating everything. The horizontal and vertical merge and challenge the blowing winds from east to west, from north to south, joined in the plenitude of a union without oblivion.

Everything here is an Elsewhere.

I invoke the new dawn nestling in the aurora, aurora surrendering to the impetus of day, silently proclaiming the advent of the sun king. I invoke the glory of the scintillating monarch, escorted by the invisible, advancing on an invincible chariot whose light is the archer, and the infinite, its target.

I invoke the fiery eye opening between Heaven and Earth, in their center enthroned the way the heart reigns at the core of being. I invoke its visionary flame, without which all is only orphan shadows, haunted by the dark orb of ghostly skies.

I invoke its splendorous displays that swallow us in solitude — where nothing is lacking, where nothing is excluded — and echo the memory of a plenitude to be resurrected. I invoke the star from elsewhere bearing the blueprint for enlightenment and fire, and the light of the whole world within.

I invoke the music of the spheres engraved on the golden disc's infinite grooves: I invoke the sun's soul and its great, still unheard love cry.

I invoke the original lovers, Heaven and Earth, their bodies touching and merging until indivisible at the end of the horizon. I invoke the inexhaustible progenitor, the rod from beyond the grave whose embrace resurrects, its demiurgic waters bathing the naked body of this world.

I invoke Earth swallowing the heavenly seed, the tireless waves washing over her hips, Life plummeting from the Infinite like a meteor shower. I invoke the million wings lifting Earth, the flight offered to platitudes here below, the contagious fervor of high winds inhaling us in their Lung and propelling us in the immensity.

I invoke heaven's seal that is Breath, indomitable Breath, Breath that pierces, purifies, resuscitates all it embraces in its elusive dance; and the fiery bush burning our finiteness, our servitudes and our dust, to reawaken in its heart, freed from space and time, their laws rendered powerless.

When all seems gone, the black night's Truth remains in the time of celestial assimilations, the great luminaries contemplating one another, eyes closed. The invisible Seer remains, the one nameless Being transcending all images.

Memory and path remain: a spark through the thread of an oblique beam back to the Sun; a pilgrim retracing the sky's fingerprints to their invisible source; a tightrope walker on razor's edge between mirror and veil of inner being; a soul in exile scampering against the void and running into the arms of Love.

The echo of silence remains, arising *in defiance of the night*, so the promise of return can vibrate and resound in the heart of stateless souls who know they don't belong here, nor elsewhere, and even less now.

AFTERWORD

A meteor has recently crossed the French poetic space: Gabriel Arnou-Laujeac. *Beyond Elsewhere* has been greeted by a burst of praise from major names in the French literary world. The French publish a lot of poetry but few works get noticed in literary journals. How can we explain such a phenomenon?

What is surprising at first is the strange tone of his book, an evocative resonance of the gap between music, painting and words. Its musicality is that of psalms and cantatas. The pictorial structure is close to that of William Blake. Words, by a secret alchemy, transcend themselves, beyond what is said in the infinite space of silence. Unclassifiable, Gabriel Arnou-Laujeac's poem-story nevertheless belongs to the spiritual family that encompasses Rumi and Michel Camus.

The second surprising fact is the feeling of total authenticity and organicity. With Arnou-Laujeac, spiritual experience precedes the poetic experience. Of great philosophical potential, his text can be attached to any philosophy. It describes the soul's journey toward the absolute sun deity common to all religions. Ultimately, the metaphysics of Gabriel Arnou-Laujeac is not intellectual; it is experimental. The readers have the impression of being a duplication of the poet, their spiritual bodies certainly tied to their physical ones, allowing them direct perception without mediation of Reality.

"Before disappearing far off, farther than the human eye could launch its arrow, the gods shook the firmament, let fall a few fragments of infinity on my forehead, and breathed the nostalgia of the Absolute into my core. A blazing firebrand planted in the soft flesh, from birth: echoes of silence striking my chest; presence within absence, sprung from the ocean of ages like a wave of equinox" writes Gabriel Arnou-Laujeac. The presence of absence is felt throughout the entire text. What is, at the beginning of the story, absence of a physical body, turns out to actually be an ardent and constant presence of the spiritual body. For two bodies united in our earthly existence, presence appears as a shadow of absence. The white light does not allow the vision of presence. Only the sun's black light allows this absolute vision. "Wherever I turned my face, I only saw a world of shadowy temples and the specter of the absence covering every atom of the universe."

Humanity's great sin is sleep, blindness to the presence, diving into oblivion, that's the true spiritual death. "Everything was too ugly to be true. I prayed to be torn from Man's long sleep (...) I would have liked the seemingly real to fall like a veil at the foot of a larger Reality, to burn there on the spot: forever."

In his path to enlightenment, the poet is inhabited, in his younger years, by "Dreams of Elsewhere. Dreams of beyond elsewhere. My lungs were seeking the high seas air, the one that is sorely lacking."

"Why doesn't passion escape the tidal movement, the law of opposites, the back and forth between shadow and light, the imperturbable mechanical decline of all things here below?" ponders Gabriel Arnou-Laujeac in one of the decisive passages of the story. The key to any truth seeker's journey is going beyond the law of opposites.

"I seek nothing, nothing known, nothing earthly. Celestial bodies, shooting stars, migratory breaths crossing the night without a trace. I seek nothing — everything — instant thousand faces never growing old, diverse bodies and gazes to deceive the emptiness of each." A terrestrial being nevertheless, the poet wanders in the desert of the world. "The absurd spreads its wings in the cage of existence. Its breath attempts to infiltrate the loophole of the body, seeking to possess me from the inside and make me the invalid priest of its inverted cult..." But he resists "its misleading vertigo, its lying mirrors" and, standing "beyond the borders of nothingness, outstretched toward the inaccessible," remembers "the All Other. It was Me."

Love acquires a liturgical dimension. "I know a paradise that is a gateway to the stars, where one can drink the sun's blood, where one staggers naked on the back of constellations. I speak to you about over there, the horizon at the end of the shadow: toward clarity. Come. I hold the keys to another world: a solar dynasty triumphing over the arbitrary triumphs as well over dust." Human love becomes a prayer for love everywhere in the cosmos. "I invoke the original lovers, Heaven and Earth, their bodies touching and merging until indivisible at the end of the horizon."

—Basarab Nicolescu

Basarab Nicolescu is a French physicist and scholar, recipient of the Prix de l'Académie Française, member of the Romanian Academy, president and founder of the International Center for Transdisciplinary Research and Studies (CIRET), co-founder of the Study Group on Transdisciplinarity at UNESCO, and author of twenty books.

Excerpted from *3è Millénaire*, translated from the French by Hélène Cardona.

Gabriel Arnou-Laujeac graduated from Sciences Po (Institute of Political Studies) and holds a Research Master's in Human Rights (Fondements des Droits de l'Homme). He has been published in many literary & philosophical journals and anthologies, notably *Les Citadelles, Poésie Directe, Littérales, Polyglotte, Recours au Poème, Testament, 3è Millénaire, L'Opinion indépendante, Petite anthologie de la jeune poésie française* (Éditions Géhess), and *Le livre de la prière* (Éditions de l'Inférieur). He also contributed to the book *Irak, la faute* (Éditions du Cerf).
A Romanian translation of *Plus loin qu'ailleurs* was published by Junimea Editions in 2014, with Spanish and Persian translations forthcoming.

   Gabriel studied Western philosophy and Indian classical philosophy with traditional Acharyas (Hindu scholars).

Hélène Cardona is a poet, literary translator and actor, whose most recent books are *Life in Suspension* (Salmon Poetry), *Dreaming My Animal Selves* (Salmon Poetry), and *Ce que nous portons* (Éditions du Cygne), her translation of Dorianne Laux. She also translated Whitman's War Writings for WhitmanWeb.

She wrote her thesis on Henry James for her Master's in English & American Literature from the Sorbonne, taught at Hamilton College and Loyola Marymount University, and received fellowships from the Goethe-Institut & Universidad Internacional de Andalucía.

She co-edits *Fulcrum: An Anthology of Poetry and Aesthetics*, is a contributor to *The London Magazine*, and co-producer of the documentary *Pablo Neruda: The Poet's Calling*. Publications include *Washington Square, Poetry International, Irish Literary Times, The Warwick Review, Plume, World Literature Today* & more.